The Sounds of TRASH

by Susan Evento

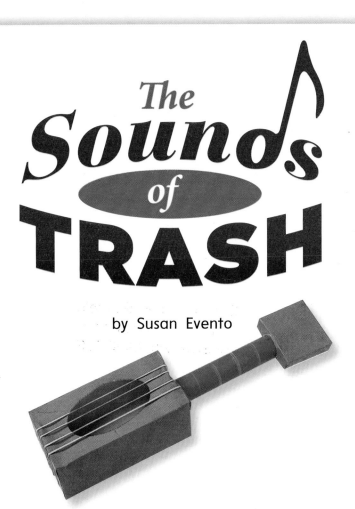

Art is one way to show how you feel.

Do you draw or paint?
Do you dance or **act**?

Singing is one way to share your feelings.

Do you sing? Do you play an **instrument**? These are ways to **express** yourself.

You can make things with trash.

You can use trash like
bottles and tubes to
express yourself!
How can you do that?

4

A bottle can be an instrument.

They can be recycled.
You can use them to make
instruments!

STOP AND CHECK

How can you use recycled
things to express yourself?

5

How to Make a Guitar

What you need:

- a shoebox with a lid
- scissors
- tape
- 4 rubber bands

What to do:

1. Cut a hole in the box lid. Get an adult to help.

2. Tape the lid onto the box.

3. Stretch the rubber bands around the box. Put them over the hole.

Pluck the rubber bands.
They move, or **vibrate**.
That makes the **sound**
you hear.

Use thin and thick
rubber bands.
They will make
different sounds.

STOP AND CHECK

What part of the guitar
makes sound?

7

How to Make a Trombone

What you need:

- 2 cardboard tubes (one should fit tightly inside the other)
- paper, scissors, and tape

What to do:

1. Make a paper cone. Tape it closed. Cut off the small end of the cone. This makes a hole.

2. Put the big tube into the hole. Tape them together.

3. Place the smaller tube inside the larger tube (the end without the cone).

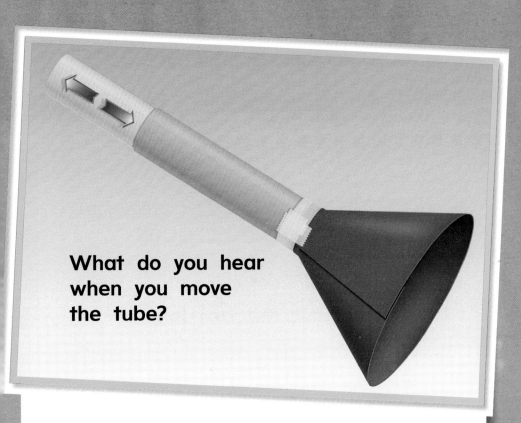

What do you hear when you move the tube?

Press your lips on the smaller tube. Make a humming sound. Move the tube up and down.

STOP AND CHECK

How can you make a sound with your trombone?

9

How to Make Maracas

What you need:

- 2 small plastic bottles with tops
- rice or dry beans

What to do:

1. Fill each bottle with beans or rice.
2. Put the caps on tightly.

Shake the maracas. The beans or rice will hit the sides of the bottles.

How to Make Drums

What you need:

- coffee can with plastic lid
- 2 pencils
- 2 erasers

What to do:

1. Put the lid on the can.
2. Put the erasers on the pencils.

When you hit a drum, it vibrates.

Hit the can with the pencils. Hit the plastic side. Hit the metal side. How are the sounds different?

13

You can play instruments with other kids. Play along to music or make your own songs. Put on a **concert**.

Express yourself!

STOP AND CHECK

How do you make sounds with maracas and drums?

It is fun to play instruments.

Respond to Reading

Summarize

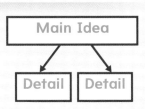

Summarize *The Sounds of Trash*. The chart may help you.

Text Evidence

1. What is the main idea of this story? Main Idea and Key Details

2. Find the word *stretch* on page 6. How can you tell what *stretch* means? Vocabulary

3. Write about an instrument you can make with trash. Use details from the story.

   Write About Reading

Compare Texts

How do people communicate through sound?

Talking Underwater

People can't talk underwater. So scuba divers make signals with their hands.

Signals help divers stay safe.

17

People's voices cannot travel through water. The signal can.

But now there is a new device. It lets divers talk underwater. The device turns a diver's voice into a signal.

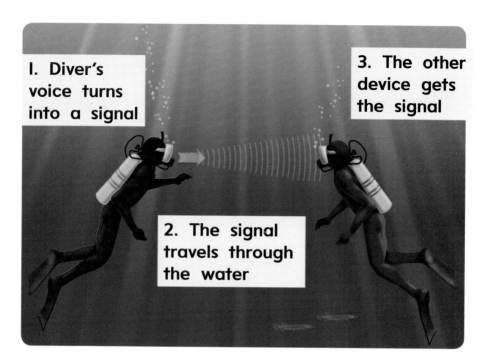

1. Diver's voice turns into a signal

3. The other device gets the signal

2. The signal travels through the water

This is how a voice can travel through water.

The signal travels from one diver to the other. The signals are turned into sounds they can understand.

Make Connections

What might you communicate underwater? Essential Question

How could you signal with instruments? Text to Text

Focus on
Science

Purpose To make an instrument with things you can find

What to Do

Step 1 ▶ Work with a partner. Think of an instrument you want to make.

Step 2 ▶ Find things you can use to make your instrument. Now make it.

Conclusion Share your instrument with the class. Explain how it makes sounds.